Budgeting Tips For Couples

Simple Steps to Manage Finances in Marriage: A Practical Guide for Both Young Couples and Old Couples

Joseph I. Kline

Copyright © (2024) (Joseph I. Kline)

All rights reserved.

No part of this publication may be reproduced, distributed, or transmitted in any form or by any means, including photocopying, recording, or other electronic or mechanical methods, without the prior written permission of us the publisher, except in the case of brief quotations embodied in critical reviews and certain other non-commercial uses permitted by copyright law.

Table of Contents

Introduction
- Why Budgeting Together Strengthens Relationships
- Money Matters: The Conversation Every Couple Needs to Have
- Setting the Foundation: Building a Financial Partnership

Chapter 1: Understanding Your Money Personalities
- How Our Upbringing Shapes Our Financial Habits
- Spender vs. Saver: Finding Balance in Different Approaches
- Recognizing Triggers: What Makes You Spend or Save?
- Aligning Goals Despite Different Money Styles

Chapter 2: Setting Financial Goals as a Couple
- Short-Term, Medium-Term, and Long-Term Goals
- Dreaming Together: Planning for the Future You Both Want
- How to Prioritize: Balancing Fun and Responsibility
- Avoiding the "One-Person-Decision" Trap

Chapter 3: Creating a Couple's Budget
- Taking Stock: Understanding Your Joint Income and Expenses
- The Reality Check: Identifying Non-Negotiables and Splurges
- Monthly, Yearly, and Seasonal Adjustments
- Using Tools and Apps: Modern Ways to Stay on Track

Chapter 4: Navigating Shared and Individual Expenses
- What Should Be Joint? What Should Be Separate?
- Respecting Individual Spending Freedom
- Managing Unequal Incomes: Fairness Without Resentment
- Dealing with Debt: Tackling It Together

Chapter 5: Planning for Major Life Changes
- Marriage, Moving In, or Starting a Family
- Buying a Home: The Biggest Budget Conversation
- Saving for Kids, Retirement, and Everything in Between
- The Unexpected: Budgeting for Emergencies and Surprises

Chapter 6: Handling Financial Setbacks Together
- Coping with Job Loss or Income Reduction
- How to Support Each Other Through Financial Stress
- Revisiting the Budget in Tough Times
- When to Seek Outside Help: Financial Advisors and Therapists

Chapter 7: Maintaining Flexibility
- The Importance of Revisiting Your Budget Regularly
- Staying Adaptable as Life Changes
- Avoiding Budget Fatigue: How to Keep It Sustainable
- Knowing When It's Time to Reward Yourselves

Conclusion
- The Peace of Mind That Comes with Financial Harmony
- Trust, Communication, and the Power of Shared Goals
- Your Path Forward: Continuing the Conversation

Introduction

Money. It's one of those things we all deal with, but somehow, when you're in a relationship, it becomes a little more complicated. Whether you've just moved in together, recently tied the knot, or have been partners for years, managing finances as a couple isn't always easy. And yet, it's one of the most important aspects of any relationship.

For many couples, talking about money feels uncomfortable. Maybe one of you is a saver, and the other loves to splurge a bit. Or perhaps you both have similar financial habits, but life keeps throwing unexpected expenses your way, making it tough to stay on track. Whatever your situation, one thing is clear: when you work together on your finances, it can bring a sense of peace and understanding that spills over into other areas of your relationship.

In this book, we're not going to focus on giving you a "one-size-fits-all" budget or telling you to cut out every little thing that brings you joy. Instead, we'll walk you through real, practical steps that help you and your partner communicate better, understand each other's financial habits, and create a budget that works for both of you.

You'll learn how to set financial goals together, balance shared and individual expenses, and adjust your budget as life changes. And if you're thinking this sounds boring or restrictive, don't worry—we'll also show you how to keep fun, spontaneity, and even a few splurges in your life, all while staying financially responsible.

Budgeting as a couple isn't just about the numbers on a spreadsheet. It's about building trust, learning to compromise, and understanding what truly matters to both of you. And the great thing? When you've got your financial life in sync, everything else tends to fall into place a little easier.

So, let's dive in. Whether you're just starting to budget together or looking to fine-tune what you've already got in place, this book will help you build a stronger financial foundation for your relationship—and maybe even bring you closer along the way.

Chapter 1

Understanding Your Money
Personalities

How Our Upbringing Shapes Our Financial Habits

The Grocery Store Epiphany

Sarah and Daniel had been married for just over a year. They were still learning how to navigate life together—figuring out who did the dishes, whose turn it was to take out the trash, and how to manage their combined finances. It was this last one, though, that always seemed to lead to tension.

One Saturday afternoon, they found themselves at the grocery store, pushing a cart through the aisles. Sarah was carefully adding up the prices in her head, picking up store-brand items, and calculating whether they could stretch the week's budget a little further. Daniel, on the other hand, had casually thrown in a couple of imported cheeses and a bottle of wine. She tried to hold back her frustration, but it was bubbling up.

As they walked down the snack aisle, Sarah finally sighed and said, "Do we really need the fancy cheese? Or the wine? We've got a budget, Daniel."

Daniel looked confused. "It's just a couple of things. I don't see the big deal. We can afford it."

"That's not the point," Sarah said, her voice tense. "We agreed to stick to the budget, but every time we shop, you just grab whatever you feel like. It's like you don't even think about it."

Now Daniel was getting defensive. "What's the problem, Sarah? We're not broke. I grew up with my parents buying things like this all the time. It's not like we're splurging on something crazy."

Sarah stopped pushing the cart and turned to face him. "Exactly. That's your family. Mine was different. My mom had to stretch every dollar just to make sure we had food on the table. I'm not saying you can't enjoy things, but I get anxious when I see us spending more than we planned. It just doesn't feel right."

Daniel blinked, realizing for the first time that they weren't just arguing over groceries. He was about to respond, but he could see how much this was affecting her. Sarah wasn't upset about the cheese or the wine—she was reacting to years of watching her mother struggle to make ends meet. Meanwhile, Daniel had grown up in a middle-class household where his parents never seemed to worry about money.

"I didn't know that," Daniel said quietly. "I guess I never thought about where we're both coming from. For me, spending a little extra on something small is no big deal, but I didn't realize it makes you feel stressed."

Sarah softened. "I don't want to make you feel like we can't ever enjoy things. I just need to know that we're being smart about it, you know? It's not about denying ourselves. It's about making sure we're on the same page."

Daniel nodded, suddenly feeling the weight of his assumptions. "Let's talk about this more when we get home. I think we need to figure out a balance that works for both of us. But, for now," he smiled gently, "let's put back the cheese and grab the cheaper one."

Sarah smiled back, relieved that they were finally starting to understand each other.

As they continued shopping, they both realized that this wasn't just about budgeting—it was about learning how their pasts shaped their views on money and finding a way forward together.

*****

How Our Upbringing Shapes Our Financial Habits

When it comes to money, the way we handle it today is often a reflection of how we grew up. Whether we realize it or not, the financial habits we develop as adults are deeply influenced by what we saw, heard, and experienced during childhood. Maybe you watched your parents diligently save every penny, or perhaps they lived paycheck to paycheck, constantly stressed about bills. These early experiences create lasting impressions, shaping how we think and feel about money.

For some, money might have been a source of comfort and security—something that was always there and never a worry. Others might have grown up in homes where financial struggles were a constant topic of conversation, making money feel like a source of anxiety. And then, there are those who grew up in families where money simply wasn't discussed. Maybe your parents handled the finances quietly behind the scenes, and you never really thought about where the money came from or how it was spent.

These early experiences don't just fade away when we grow up. If you're the child of savers, you might feel a strong urge to build up your savings, even if it means sacrificing things you enjoy. On the flip side, if you grew up in a household where spending freely was the norm, you might find it difficult to say no to purchases, even when your budget is tight. Neither approach is inherently good or bad, but understanding where your habits come from can help you and your partner find common ground.

When two people from different financial backgrounds come together, there's often a learning curve. Maybe you grew up in a home where your parents argued about money, and now you find yourself avoiding financial discussions because they feel uncomfortable. Or perhaps you're used to handling your own finances and find it challenging to share that responsibility with someone else.

The main point is to identify these patterns without passing judgment. We all carry a bit of our upbringing into adulthood, and that includes our attitudes toward money. Being aware of how those early experiences shape your current habits is very important and it will be good to have open conversations with your partner about where you're both coming from.

Understanding each other's financial backgrounds can help you make sense of why you approach money the way you do. It's not about who's right or wrong; it's about learning to blend your different experiences and perspectives to create a financial strategy that works for both of you. After all, once you're aware of where your habits come from, you can start making choices that reflect the life you want to build together—not just the one you were raised in.

Spender vs. Saver: Finding Balance in Different Approaches

In almost every relationship, there's usually one person who loves to save and another who enjoys spending a bit more freely. Maybe one of you gets a thrill out of finding a great deal and tucking money away for the future, while the other feels that life's too short not to enjoy the moment and splurge a little now and then. Neither way is wrong, but these differences can lead to some friction if not managed well.

Take Amanda and Josh, for example. Amanda was the classic saver. She loved the sense of security that came with having a healthy savings account and always looked for ways to cut back on unnecessary expenses. Josh, on the other hand, was more of a "live in the moment" type. He believed that money was meant to be enjoyed, whether that meant going out to eat or upgrading his tech gadgets.

This difference didn't seem like a big deal at first, but over time, they noticed how it impacted their relationship. Amanda would get anxious whenever Josh suggested a spontaneous weekend getaway or bought something that wasn't planned for in the budget. Josh, meanwhile, felt frustrated, like he had to justify every little thing he wanted to spend money on.

The challenge for couples like Amanda and Josh isn't about trying to change the other person's approach but rather finding a balance. Both spending and saving have their benefits. Savers help build financial stability, while spenders remind us that it's okay to enjoy life along the way. The trick is learning to appreciate what the other person brings to the table and figuring out a middle ground that works for both of you.

For Amanda and Josh, it meant creating a budget that allowed for saving while also setting aside a "fun fund" for the occasional splurge. This way, Amanda could feel secure knowing they were still saving for the future, and Josh didn't feel guilty about enjoying the present. They also agreed to talk openly about larger purchases beforehand, so no one felt blindsided.

Here, we are not trying to force the spender to become a strict saver or the saver to throw caution to the wind. It's about understanding each other's priorities and finding a way to blend them so that both of you feel comfortable with your financial decisions. When you start to work together like this, money stops being a source of tension and becomes part of building the life you both want.

Recognizing Triggers: What Makes You Spend or Save?

We all have those moments when we make money decisions without even realizing why. Maybe you're feeling stressed after a tough day at work, so you treat yourself to something you don't really need. Or perhaps you grew up in a household where money was tight, and now you feel a strong urge to save every extra penny, even when you're in a good financial place. The truth is, we're often triggered by emotions or past experiences that shape how we handle money.

Take Emily, for example. Whenever she felt overwhelmed at work, she found herself browsing online stores, looking for something—anything—that would give her a little pick-me-up. A new pair of shoes, a kitchen gadget, even a fancy candle. She didn't always need these things, but the act of buying them made her feel in control, at least for a moment.

Her partner, Mark, was the opposite. He grew up in a family where money was tight, so saving gave him a sense of security. He felt uneasy when their bank account dipped below a certain amount, even if they had more than enough to cover their bills. Mark's "trigger" was fear—fear of not having enough, even when things were fine.

Recognizing these triggers can be a game-changer for couples. Once you're aware of what drives your spending or saving habits, you can start to manage them instead of letting them control you. For Emily, realizing that stress was driving her impulse buys helped her find healthier ways to cope, like taking a walk or calling a friend. For Mark, understanding that his fear of running out of money was rooted in his past allowed him to ease up a bit and enjoy the present.

You have to be honest with yourself—and with each other—about what triggers your financial habits. Are you spending to fill an emotional gap? Or are you saving out of fear rather than necessity? When you can pinpoint what's really going on, you and your partner can make smarter choices that fit your financial goals and emotional needs.

Talking openly about these triggers with your partner can also build empathy. Once Mark understood that Emily's spending wasn't just about wanting more "stuff" but was tied to her stress, he was more supportive when they worked on their budget together. And when Emily realized that Mark's desire to save was more about feeling secure, she stopped pushing him to spend on things that didn't matter to him.

Recognizing what makes you spend or save is the first step to creating a balanced approach to money—one that considers both your emotional triggers and your financial goals.

Aligning Goals Despite Different Money Styles

When two people come together, it's natural that they'll have different approaches to money. One of you might focus on building savings and planning for the future, while the other enjoys spending on experiences or things that make life fun in the moment. These different money styles can lead to friction, especially when it comes to setting long-term goals, but the good news is that it's entirely possible to find common ground.

The first step is understanding that neither approach is inherently wrong. One person's desire to save comes from a place of security—they want to make sure there's a safety net for whatever life throws their way. On the other hand, the one who enjoys spending may prioritize living in the present, valuing experiences or purchases that bring immediate joy. Both perspectives have value, and together, they can create a more balanced financial life.

To align your goals, it's important to have open conversations about what you both want. What are your dreams, both individually and as a couple? Whether it's buying a house, traveling more, starting a family, or simply having a comfortable retirement, laying out your goals allows you to see where you're aligned and where you might need to compromise. It's not about convincing the other person to abandon their money style—it's about blending your approaches so that both short-term enjoyment and long-term security are part of the plan.

At this point, create a budget that reflects both priorities. Set aside money for the things that bring joy now, while also making sure you're saving for the future. Maybe it's allocating a portion of your income to an emergency fund or retirement, but also setting up a fund for fun experiences or treats. This way, neither person feels deprived, and both of your values are respected.

Communication is crucial in this process. Regularly check in with each other to see how you're feeling about your financial progress. Are you both still on track toward your shared goals? Are there any adjustments that need to be made? Keeping the conversation going helps avoid misunderstandings and ensures that both of you feel heard and involved in your financial journey.

The real challenge in aligning goals isn't changing each other's money styles; it's about embracing your differences and using them to build a future that reflects both of your values. When you do that, money becomes less of a source of tension and more of a tool to help you create the life you want together.

Chapter 2

Setting Financial Goals as a Couple

Short-Term, Medium-Term, and Long-Term Goals

When it comes to managing finances, setting goals is essential. But not all goals are created equal, and recognizing the difference between short-term, medium-term, and long-term objectives can make a significant impact on your financial planning. Each type of goal plays a unique role in your overall strategy, and understanding how they fit together can help you stay focused and motivated.

Short-term goals: These are typically the easiest to identify. These are the things you want to achieve within the next year or so. They often involve immediate needs or desires—maybe saving for a vacation, paying off a small debt, or even building an emergency fund. Since these goals are relatively quick to accomplish, they provide a sense of immediate gratification and can motivate you to stay on track with your finances. Tracking your progress on these goals can give you quick wins, reinforcing positive financial behaviors.

Medium-term goals: These types of goals stretch a bit further into the future, typically ranging from one to five years. These goals require a bit more planning and commitment. They might include saving for a new car, a major home renovation, or a significant vacation that requires a larger budget. These goals can often feel more substantial, and achieving them usually involves a combination of saving and budgeting over a longer period. Because they take time, medium-term goals can help you build patience and discipline, reinforcing the importance of planning for your future while still enjoying your present.

Long-term goals: long-term goals usually extend beyond five years. These goals often require significant financial commitment and foresight. They might include saving for retirement, buying a home, or funding your children's education. Long-term goals can sometimes feel daunting, as they require sustained effort over many years. However, they are also incredibly rewarding when you see the results of your planning and hard work. By establishing these goals, you create a roadmap for your future that helps guide your financial decisions today.

To effectively manage your finances, it's essential to have a mix of these goals. Each type serves a different purpose and helps maintain balance in your financial life. When you focus on short-term goals, you can enjoy immediate satisfaction, while medium-term goals teach you to plan and save for more significant purchases. Long-term goals provide a sense of direction, encouraging you to think about your future and make decisions that align with your values.

As you work together to set these goals, keep in mind that flexibility is crucial. Life can be unpredictable, and you may need to adjust your goals along the way. Regularly revisiting your financial objectives as a couple allows you to stay aligned and make changes as needed, ensuring that your goals evolve with your lives.

Setting short-term, medium-term, and long-term goals creates a comprehensive financial plan that reflects your priorities as a couple. By clearly defining what you want to achieve at different stages of your life, you can better navigate the complexities of managing your finances and enjoy the journey along the way.

Dreaming Together: Planning for the Future You Both Want

When two people commit to each other, they often start to envision a future together. However, it's not just about the big milestones like getting married or buying a house; it's also about the dreams and aspirations that shape your life as a couple. Planning for the future you both want involves more than just logistics and numbers—it's about creating a shared vision that reflects both of your values and desires.

To begin this process, it's essential to have open and honest conversations about what you each want. What are your individual dreams? Do you envision traveling the world, starting a family, or pursuing a particular career path? Sharing these thoughts creates a deeper understanding of each other's priorities and helps you align your goals. This exchange can be incredibly enriching, revealing not only your aspirations but also the motivations behind them.

Once you've shared your dreams, the next step is to discuss how you can bring those visions to life together. This might involve financial planning, but it also requires emotional investment and commitment to supporting each other. It's important to recognize that some goals may require compromise and collaboration. For instance, if one person dreams of living in a bustling city while the other prefers a quieter suburban life, finding a middle ground may become part of the planning process.

As you work together, consider creating a shared vision board or writing down your goals. Visual representations can serve as powerful reminders of what you're working toward and keep you both motivated. This tangible display of your dreams can inspire you to take actionable steps and keep your focus on the bigger picture.

Remember, planning for the future is not a one-time discussion; it's an ongoing conversation. Life evolves, and so do your dreams. Regularly revisiting your goals allows you to assess your progress, make necessary adjustments, and celebrate achievements along the way. This practice fosters a sense of teamwork and reinforces the idea that you're both in this together.

By dreaming together and actively planning for the future, you create a strong foundation for your relationship. It reinforces your connection and helps you navigate life's challenges as a united front. When you both feel invested in the journey, it transforms financial planning from a daunting task into an exciting adventure.

Ultimately, the goal is to build a life that reflects both of your dreams, where you support and uplift each other as you move toward the future you've envisioned together. Embracing this collaborative approach not only enriches your financial planning but also deepens the bond you share as partners.

How to Prioritize: Balancing Fun and Responsibility

Finding the right balance between enjoying life and being financially responsible can feel like walking a tightrope. On one hand, you want to savor experiences, create memories, and occasionally indulge in the things that bring you joy. On the other hand, you know the importance of staying on top of your responsibilities and saving for the future. So, how do you navigate this delicate dance?

The first step is understanding your values and what truly matters to both of you. Take a moment to sit down together and discuss your priorities. What do you enjoy doing as a couple? Is it dining out, traveling, or trying out new hobbies? Identifying what brings you joy can help you allocate time and resources toward those experiences while still ensuring you're meeting your obligations.

Once you've established what's important to you, it's time to create a financial plan that reflects those priorities. Consider setting aside a specific portion of your budget for fun activities or experiences. This "fun fund" allows you to indulge without guilt, knowing that you're still covering your essential expenses and saving for future goals. By having a designated amount for leisure, you can enjoy your time together without constantly worrying about how it affects your financial health.

It's also crucial to regularly reassess your priorities and be open to adjustments. Life is full of surprises, and sometimes circumstances change. Perhaps a new opportunity arises that requires a shift in your budget, or maybe you discover a new passion that you want to explore. Being flexible allows you to adapt your plans without sacrificing your enjoyment.

Another helpful approach is to find ways to combine fun with responsibility. For instance, instead of always dining out, consider hosting a potluck with friends or trying a new recipe at home. You can still enjoy socializing and create memorable moments without straying too far from your budget. Look for free or low-cost activities in your community, such as local events, festivals, or outdoor activities. Often, the best experiences don't require a hefty price tag.

Ultimately, balancing fun and responsibility is about finding harmony. It's not about cutting out the joys of life completely; rather, it's about making conscious choices that align with your values. When you prioritize both aspects, you create a fulfilling life that includes cherished experiences while ensuring a secure financial future.

Regularly checking in with each other about how you're feeling regarding your balance is also essential. Are you satisfied with how you're managing fun and responsibility? Open dialogue fosters understanding and helps you navigate any concerns that arise. By working together, you can support each other in maintaining that balance, turning it into an ongoing journey rather than a rigid task.

In the end, the goal is to enjoy life while being mindful of your responsibilities. When you strike this balance, you create a healthy financial dynamic that enhances your relationship and enriches your shared experiences.

Avoiding the "One-Person-Decision" Trap

In any relationship, it's easy to fall into the habit of making decisions independently, especially when it comes to finances. You might find yourself thinking, "I'll just handle this on my own," believing that it's quicker or simpler. However, this approach can lead to misunderstandings, resentment, and a feeling of disconnect over time. Avoiding the "one-person-decision" trap is crucial for fostering a healthy partnership and ensuring that both of your voices are heard.

The first step in breaking this pattern is to recognize that financial decisions affect both of you. Even seemingly small choices, like what to buy for the house or whether to sign up for a subscription service, can have a ripple effect on your budget and shared goals. Taking the time to discuss these decisions together not only promotes transparency but also strengthens your connection as a couple.

Make it a habit to involve each other in discussions about finances, regardless of the size of the decision. Create a space where both of you feel comfortable expressing your opinions and concerns. This collaborative approach allows you to weigh the pros and cons together, ensuring that you're aligned in your financial strategy. Plus, it encourages a sense of teamwork that's essential for a healthy relationship.

When discussing financial decisions, aim for open communication. Instead of making a decision unilaterally and then presenting it as a fait accompli, invite your partner into the conversation. For example, if you're considering a significant purchase, share your thoughts and rationale. Ask for their input and be open to their perspective. This collaborative dialogue fosters mutual respect and understanding.

Another effective strategy is to set aside regular time to discuss finances together. Whether it's a monthly budget review or a casual check-in about your financial goals, having these dedicated moments allows both of you to stay informed and engaged. It can also help prevent any surprises down the line, as you're both aware of your financial situation and any decisions that are being made.

Finally, be mindful of each other's feelings and viewpoints. It's natural to have different opinions on spending, saving, or investing, and that's okay. Embrace those differences as opportunities for growth and learning. Approach disagreements with curiosity rather than defensiveness. Try to understand why your partner feels strongly about a particular decision, and share your reasoning as well. This mutual exploration can lead to more balanced outcomes and a deeper understanding of each other's financial styles.

By actively working to avoid the "one-person-decision" trap, you create a financial partnership built on trust and cooperation. When both partners feel involved and valued in the decision-making process, it not only enhances your financial health but also strengthens your relationship. Ultimately, it's about building a future together, where both of your voices are integral to the journey.

Chapter 3

Creating a Couple's Budget

Taking Stock: Understanding Our Joint Income and Expenses

Navigating finances as a couple can feel overwhelming at times, especially when we come from different backgrounds and have varied experiences with money. However, taking stock of our joint income and expenses doesn't have to be stressful. In fact, I've found that it can be an enlightening experience that strengthens our partnership and helps us work toward our shared financial goals.

The first step in this journey is to sit down together and have an open conversation about our financial situation. We start by discussing all sources of income, whether it's salaries, freelance work, or side hustles. Being transparent about our earnings creates a clear picture of our financial landscape and sets the stage for effective budgeting.

Next, we tackle our expenses. We create a list of all our regular monthly costs—rent or mortgage, utilities, groceries, and transportation. We make sure to include irregular expenses, like annual subscriptions or insurance premiums. Being comprehensive in this process gives us a complete view of where our money is going, and it often reveals spending habits that we may not have been fully aware of.

As we categorize our expenses, we distinguish between needs and wants. Needs are the essentials—things we can't live without—while wants are the extra comforts or luxuries that enhance our lives but aren't strictly necessary. Understanding this distinction helps us prioritize our spending and align our financial choices with our shared goals.

Once we have a clear picture of our income and expenses, we discuss our financial goals together. What do we envision for our future? Whether it's buying a home, saving for travel, or planning for retirement, aligning our financial priorities is crucial. Knowing what we're working toward makes it easier to find ways to adjust our spending and savings.

We also make it a point to regularly review our financial situation. We set aside time each month to go over our income and expenses, discussing any changes or unexpected costs. This practice keeps us informed about our financial health and encourages accountability and teamwork. It's an opportunity to celebrate our wins—both big and small—and to make adjustments as needed.

Throughout this process, I remind myself that finances are just one aspect of our relationship.

While it's essential to have these conversations, we keep the tone constructive and supportive. I approach discussions with curiosity rather than judgment, recognizing that we both bring unique perspectives to the table. Creating an environment where we both feel safe expressing our thoughts and concerns is vital for maintaining a healthy dialogue around money.

Taking stock of our joint income and expenses is more than just a financial exercise; it's a step toward building a stronger partnership. By understanding our financial situation together, we create a solid foundation for navigating our future as a team. With transparency, regular communication, and a shared vision, we can tackle any financial challenges that come our way and enjoy the journey together.

The Reality Check: Identifying Non-Negotiables and Splurges

When it comes to managing finances as a couple, one of the most important steps is understanding what truly matters to both of you. This involves taking a good, hard look at your spending habits and identifying what can't be compromised versus what you can indulge in from time to time. This reality check can help create a financial roadmap that aligns with your values and strengthens your partnership.

To begin, I suggest having an open and honest discussion about your non-negotiables. These are the essentials—expenses or experiences that you consider vital for your well-being and happiness. They might include things like housing, healthcare, or even regular date nights that nurture your relationship. Recognizing these non-negotiables allows you to prioritize them in your budget, ensuring that your essential needs are met without causing unnecessary stress.

Next, it's equally important to identify your splurges—those little indulgences that bring joy and add a spark to your everyday life. These might be things like dining out, weekend getaways, or even a subscription to a favorite streaming service. By pinpointing what you genuinely enjoy and value, you can allocate funds to these areas without guilt. It's all about balance; when you know what you want to treat yourselves to, it becomes easier to make room for those pleasures within your overall budget.

One effective way to approach this conversation is to write down your non-negotiables and splurges separately. Discussing and comparing your lists can reveal areas of overlap as well as differences. For instance, you might both agree that having quality time together is a non-negotiable, while one of you sees value in investing in experiences like travel, while the other prefers to splurge on home entertainment. Understanding each other's priorities opens up avenues for compromise and collaboration.

Once you've established your lists, consider how they fit into your broader financial goals. Are there any splurges that you can temporarily cut back on to prioritize a non-negotiable? Perhaps you can scale down on takeout in order to save for a much-desired vacation. These conversations are about finding that sweet spot where both partners feel their needs and desires are acknowledged and respected.

It's also helpful to periodically revisit these lists. Life changes—new job opportunities, growing families, or shifting interests—can impact what feels essential versus what is a nice-to-have. By checking in with each other regularly, you can ensure that your budget remains aligned with your evolving priorities.

Ultimately, this reality check about non-negotiables and splurges is not just about crunching numbers; it's a way to deepen your understanding of each other. It fosters communication and helps build trust in your financial partnership. When both of you feel secure in knowing that your core needs are met while still allowing for some enjoyable indulgences, you create a healthier and more satisfying financial life together.

Monthly, Yearly, and Seasonal Adjustments

Managing a household budget is more of a journey than a destination; it requires ongoing attention and a willingness to adapt. Rather than treating your finances as a static plan, embracing the idea of monthly, yearly, and seasonal adjustments can help you create a flexible financial roadmap that meets your needs and goals.

Monthly adjustments are about staying in tune with the here and now. Each month brings its own set of expenses, whether it's bills, groceries, or unexpected costs. At the beginning of every month, my partner and I make it a point to sit down together and review our budget. We check in on what's coming up—maybe a birthday party we forgot about or a necessary home repair we need to address. These regular check-ins allow us to adapt our spending without losing sight of our priorities.

We also take a moment to reflect on how we did the previous month. Did we stick to our budget? Were there areas where we overspent? Celebrating our wins, no matter how small, keeps us motivated.

If we managed to cut back on dining out, for instance, we use that as a springboard to explore other ways to save. Looking for patterns in our expenses helps us be more prepared for the months ahead.

When it comes to yearly adjustments, we think about the bigger picture. Certain expenses are predictable, like taxes or annual subscriptions. Knowing these costs are on the horizon helps us plan ahead, setting aside money each month so we aren't blindsided. For example, if our car insurance is due in June, we allocate a little extra each month to cover it comfortably when the time comes.

Yearly reviews also provide a valuable opportunity to reassess our financial goals. Are we on track with our savings? Have any life changes shifted our priorities? These conversations allow us to tweak our budget, ensuring it still reflects what we want for our future.

Seasonal adjustments come into play with the unique demands of different times of the year. Summer vacations, back-to-school expenses, and holiday shopping can all add up. Anticipating these seasonal costs helps us avoid the last-minute scramble to find extra funds. We create a plan that allocates money for these anticipated expenses, so when summer rolls around or the holidays approach, we feel prepared rather than overwhelmed.

Identifying these seasonal trends also gives us a chance to strategize. For instance, we might decide to cut back on discretionary spending a few months before the holiday season to make room for gift-giving without resorting to credit cards.

The real key to making these adjustments work is communication. We keep the lines open, discussing our finances regularly and being honest about any concerns. This partnership not only helps us stay on the same page but also strengthens our connection. When we both feel involved in the budgeting process, it makes adapting our plans feel like a team effort rather than a chore.

When we embrace this ongoing cycle of adjustments, we create a financial plan that's flexible and responsive to life's twists and turns. It empowers us to handle unexpected expenses while staying focused on our long-term goals. The more engaged we are in managing our budget together, the more confident we feel about our financial future as a couple.

Using Tools and Apps: Modern Ways to Stay on Track

Managing finances in today's digital age can be made significantly easier with the right tools and apps. Instead of feeling overwhelmed by budgeting, couples can utilize technology to stay organized and focused on their financial goals.

First, exploring various budgeting apps can provide options that fit individual lifestyles. There's a wide range of tools available, from simple expense trackers to comprehensive platforms that analyze spending habits. Couples can try out a few apps to find one that resonates with them, ensuring they can both input expenses and view their overall budget in real time.

One key feature in many budgeting apps is the ability to categorize spending. By labeling purchases—such as groceries, entertainment, or utilities—couples can quickly see where their money is going. This clarity often sparks discussions about spending habits and helps identify areas for potential cutbacks. For example, noticing higher-than-expected dining expenses might encourage planning more meals at home.

Automated budgeting features can also play a crucial role. Setting up alerts and reminders helps couples stay on track with their spending and savings goals. Notifications about approaching budget limits in specific categories or gentle nudges to save for upcoming expenses keep partners accountable without being overwhelming.

Shared expense trackers can enhance transparency in a relationship. These platforms allow couples to record shared costs—like groceries and utilities—making it easy to see contributions from both partners. This simplicity prevents misunderstandings and eliminates awkward conversations about who owes what.

Regularly reviewing financial apps together is another effective practice. This approach not only aligns couples on their budget but also provides an opportunity to celebrate financial wins, such as exceeding savings goals or staying within budget. Recognizing progress reinforces commitment and teamwork in managing finances.

Embracing modern tools and apps transforms budgeting from a daunting chore into an engaging part of life. With the clarity and organization these resources provide, couples can focus on what truly matters—enjoying their lives together while maintaining responsible financial practices. As technology continues to evolve, there will always be new tools to explore, further enhancing the financial journey for couples.

Here are some popular apps that can help couples manage their finances effectively:

1. Mint: This free budgeting app allows users to track expenses, create budgets, and monitor their financial goals. It automatically categorizes transactions and provides insights into spending habits.
1. 10. Zeta: Specifically designed for couples, Zeta allows partners to manage their finances together. Users can track shared expenses, set financial goals, and manage individual and joint accounts.
2. YNAB (You Need a Budget): YNAB is a budgeting tool focused on proactive financial management. It encourages users to assign every dollar a job, helping couples prioritize their spending and savings.
3. EveryDollar: Created by financial expert Dave Ramsey, this app offers a simple way to create

and manage a monthly budget. Users can track expenses and plan their budgets collaboratively.

4. PocketGuard: This app helps users see how much disposable income they have after accounting for bills, goals, and necessities. It offers insights on spending patterns and helps couples find areas to save.

5. GoodBudget: Based on the envelope budgeting method, GoodBudget allows users to allocate funds to different spending categories. It's available on multiple devices, making it easy for couples to manage their shared budget.

6. Splitwise: While not strictly a budgeting app, Splitwise is excellent for tracking shared expenses. Couples can record who paid for what and keep track of IOUs, making it easier to manage joint costs.

7. Honeydue: Designed specifically for couples, Honeydue lets partners track their finances

together. Users can see each other's transactions, set budgets, and remind one another about upcoming bills.

8. Wally: This app allows users to track expenses, set budgets, and analyze spending habits. It offers features like receipt scanning and currency conversion, making it suitable for travel as well.

9. Personal Capital: This app provides tools for budgeting and investment tracking. Couples can monitor their spending and also get insights into their retirement savings and overall financial health.

These apps offer various features and approaches to budgeting, making it easier for couples to find one that suits their needs and helps them stay on track with their financial goals.

Chapter 4

Navigating Shared and Individual Expenses

What Should Be Joint? What Should Be Separate?

When it comes to managing money as a couple, one of the biggest questions is deciding what should be handled together and what should stay separate. There's no one-size-fits-all answer, and it often depends on your relationship, your financial situation, and your individual preferences. What's most important is having an honest conversation to figure out what works best for both of you.

Joint accounts and shared expenses are common when it comes to things like rent or mortgage, utilities, groceries, and other household expenses. Pooling your money for these essentials can make it easier to manage the day-to-day running of your home. Having a joint account specifically for shared costs also provides transparency, so both partners know what's coming in and going out.

On the other hand, keeping some finances separate can offer a sense of independence and personal control, which is important in any relationship. Some couples prefer to have their own individual accounts for personal spending, like hobbies, entertainment, or small purchases. This way, you can enjoy your interests without feeling like you need to justify every dollar spent.

There's also the question of how to handle larger financial goals, such as saving for a vacation, a down payment on a house, or retirement. For some, creating joint savings accounts for these shared dreams makes sense. It allows both partners to contribute equally (or proportionally, depending on income) and work toward the same goals. Others might prefer to keep their savings separate but still agree on a strategy for reaching those goals together.

It's not just about the practical side of things, though. How you handle joint and separate finances can also influence how you feel in the relationship. For some, having everything combined strengthens the sense of unity and teamwork. For others, maintaining some financial independence can prevent conflicts and make each person feel more empowered.

Ultimately, there's no right or wrong way to split finances—it's about finding what feels fair and balanced for both of you. Some couples go all-in with fully joint finances, while others prefer a mix of shared and separate accounts. What's important is being open about your expectations and needs, discussing how you'll handle money together, and staying flexible as life changes.

It might take some trial and error to figure out what works best for your relationship. The key is to communicate regularly, check in with each other, and be willing to make adjustments as you go.

Respecting Individual Spending Freedom

Respecting personal space is essential for finding true happiness in any meaningful relationship, not just between couples but in all types of connections.

Relationships are like a bonfire: "I'll give you warmth if you stay in your space, but if you step too far into mine, you might get burned." This analogy highlights how important it is to maintain individuality within relationships. It's about creating a healthy balance where both partners can grow and thrive, while still sharing a bond.

Think of it like two overlapping circles. There's "my life" and "your life," with a shared space in the middle. The goal isn't to merge into one but to create a meaningful intersection where you can both connect while maintaining your own identities.

When each person has the freedom to explore their own interests and enjoy personal time, it strengthens the relationship. Experiencing "my space" makes you appreciate "our space" even more when you come back to it. This balance allows for deeper bonding and personal growth, as each partner can pursue what makes them happy as an individual.

Giving one another the freedom to breathe and enjoy personal space fosters a healthier connection. As the old Indian saying goes, the deeper the roots, the taller the tree. The stronger the foundation of respect for each other's individuality, the stronger the relationship will become over time.

This concept is also applicable when it comes to spending freedom between the couple.

One of the most important aspects of managing money as a couple is allowing each person the space to make their own financial decisions. Even when you're sharing finances and working together toward joint goals, maintaining a sense of independence with personal spending can help keep the peace and strengthen your relationship.

Having individual spending freedom means each partner has the ability to spend money on things they value, without feeling the need to justify every purchase. It might be something small, like buying a new book or treating yourself to a fancy coffee, or something bigger like a hobby or personal project. The point is, this freedom helps maintain a sense of individuality, which is just as important in a relationship as shared goals.

Couples can avoid friction by agreeing on a set amount of personal spending money each month.

This money is separate from joint expenses—like bills or savings—and is simply for each person to spend however they choose. It creates a clear boundary, where both partners can enjoy their own interests without questioning or scrutinizing each other's choices.

Respecting this freedom requires trust. It's not about keeping secrets but about understanding that both people in the relationship have different priorities and ways of enjoying life. Some may prefer to spend their personal money on experiences like travel or dining out with friends, while others might invest in their hobbies or save up for something special. The important thing is that neither person feels controlled or restricted.

Giving each other this financial breathing room also helps prevent resentment from building up. When every purchase has to be discussed or justified, it can feel like a lack of autonomy, which can lead to frustration. But when both partners know they have the freedom to spend within agreed limits, it brings a sense of balance and fairness to the relationship.

In the end, respecting individual spending freedom is about understanding that being part of a couple doesn't mean losing your independence. It's about blending the responsibility of managing shared finances with the personal freedom to enjoy your money in your own way. This balance helps maintain harmony and ensures both partners feel respected and trusted in their financial lives.

Dealing with Debt: Tackling It Together

Debt can be one of the most challenging things to face in a relationship, but how you handle it as a couple can either strengthen your bond or create tension. The key is approaching it as a team rather than letting it become something that divides you.

First, it's crucial to have an honest and open conversation about the debt. Whether it's student loans, credit card balances, or other financial obligations, being upfront about what each person owes helps build trust. It's not always easy to admit how much debt you're carrying, but keeping it hidden only leads to more stress down the road. When both partners know the full picture, you can begin to figure out how to tackle it together.

Once you've laid everything on the table, it's time to come up with a plan. This means sitting down and figuring out how much is owed, what the interest rates are, and how much you can afford to pay off each month. For some, it might make sense to prioritize high-interest debts first; for others, chipping away at smaller balances to gain momentum might feel more rewarding. The important thing is that you're in it together and working toward the same goal.

Dealing with debt often requires some lifestyle adjustments, and this is where teamwork really matters. It might mean cutting back on non-essential spending or putting off a vacation until you're in a better financial position. When both partners are committed to the plan, it feels less like a sacrifice and more like a shared effort to reach a better future. Knowing you're both on the same page can make those tough decisions feel a little easier.

Dealing with debt is a process. It's not going to disappear overnight, but by consistently working together, you can make steady progress. Patience, understanding, and communication are key. Some months might be harder than others, and unexpected expenses can throw off even the best-laid plans. But when you're facing it as a team, you can adjust and keep moving forward without letting it put a strain on your relationship.

Tackling debt together can actually strengthen your partnership. It teaches you how to communicate openly, solve problems as a team, and work toward common goals—all things that can bring you closer. While debt can feel overwhelming, handling it side by side shows that no financial challenge is too big to face together.

Chapter 5

Planning for Major Life Changes

Marriage, Moving In, or Starting a Family

Marriage, moving in together, or starting a family are some of the biggest steps you can take in life, and each comes with its own set of emotions, adjustments, and challenges. As exciting as these milestones are, they require a lot of communication, compromise, and planning.

When you decide to move in together, it's a significant shift, even if you've been in a long-term relationship. Living under the same roof means blending not only your routines and habits but also your personal space. Suddenly, things you might never have thought about before—like how to divide chores, share responsibilities, or even agree on what groceries to buy—become part of your daily life. It's important to approach these changes with a mindset of patience and flexibility. You're creating a home together, and that means learning how to accommodate each other's quirks and preferences while figuring out a rhythm that works for both of you.

Marriage brings an even deeper level of commitment. While living together might teach you how to co-exist, marriage often brings a more profound sense of shared responsibility. It's not just about the day-to-day logistics anymore, but about planning for the future as a team. Financial discussions become a big part of the equation, and it's important to be open about your goals, debts, and priorities. Whether it's planning for a home, saving for a big trip, or thinking long-term about retirement, aligning your vision for the future helps create a stronger foundation for your relationship.

Then there's the decision of starting a family, which is a whole new level of life change. It's a deeply personal choice that requires thoughtful conversation and careful preparation. Not only does it impact your time and energy, but it also brings financial implications that need to be considered, from medical costs to education savings and everyday expenses that come with raising a child.

In order to navigate these major life transitions, you must understand that while you're now sharing your life with someone else, it's still important to respect each other's individuality. Whether it's how you manage your personal space when you move in together, how you handle your finances as a married couple, or how you balance your own needs with the demands of raising a family, every decision requires collaboration and compromise.

These big steps—whether taken all at once or gradually—can test your relationship, but they can also deepen your connection. Facing these milestones together helps you grow not just as a couple but as individuals, making your bond stronger as you move through life's changes side by side.

Buying a Home: The Biggest Budget Conversation

Buying a home is often one of the most exciting—and nerve-wracking—financial steps a couple will take. It's not just a big purchase, it's a long-term commitment that can shape your future together in a major way. That's why it's crucial to have an open, realistic conversation about what you both want, and more importantly, what you can actually afford.

The first step in this process is figuring out your priorities. What kind of home do you see yourselves living in? Do you want something in the city close to work, or are you dreaming of a quiet place with a yard? Maybe location is less important than having a home with space for a growing family. These kinds of discussions set the stage for what you're both looking for, but they also help define what's realistic given your budget.

Once you have a rough idea of what you want, the real budgeting talk begins. It's not just about the price of the house—it's about everything that comes with it. Mortgages, down payments, property taxes, maintenance costs, and even unexpected repairs can add up fast. This is why it's essential to look at your entire financial picture, including any debt, savings, and current expenses, to figure out how much you can comfortably spend without feeling stretched too thin.

Getting pre-approved for a mortgage can help clarify what's possible. It gives you a sense of how much a bank is willing to lend you, but more importantly, it lets you know what monthly payments will look like. Just because you're approved for a certain amount doesn't mean you should max out that limit. It's all about making sure those monthly payments fit within your budget and leave room for other financial goals, like saving for the future or dealing with life's unexpected expenses.

The homebuying process can stir up some tough conversations about money. You might find one partner is more willing to stretch the budget to get a dream home, while the other prefers to stay more conservative. These differences are normal, but they need to be addressed early on. It's all about compromise and making sure you're both comfortable with the decision you're making. After all, you don't want to end up resenting the house—or each other—because you pushed yourselves too hard financially.

It's also important to think about the long-term. A home isn't just a short-term investment; it's something you'll likely be paying for over many years. Ask yourselves questions like: Will we be able to manage these payments if one of us loses a job? How will this affect our other financial goals, like retirement or starting a family? Being honest about these questions helps ensure that buying a home is a step forward, not something that adds unnecessary stress.

Buying a home is an exciting milestone, but it's also one of the biggest financial decisions a couple can make together. Having clear, honest conversations about your budget, priorities, and long-term goals will not only make the process smoother but will also help ensure that your new home is a place of joy and security—not financial strain.

*****

Imagine Sarah and David, a young couple eager to buy their first home. Sarah dreams of a spacious house in a quiet neighborhood, while David leans toward a smaller, more affordable option closer to the city. They sit down one evening to talk through their options.

Sarah points out how wonderful it would be to have room for future kids and a big backyard, but David, more focused on their budget, shares his concerns about the monthly mortgage payment, along with property taxes and maintenance costs. He wants to make sure they can still save for emergencies and take a vacation once in a while.

Together, they decide to get pre-approved for a mortgage, giving them a clearer sense of what they can actually afford. Even though the bank approves them for a larger loan, they agree to look for homes below that amount, ensuring they can comfortably make payments without stressing their budget. They compromise on a home with enough space for the future but still within walking distance of work, hitting that sweet spot between Sarah's dreams and David's practicality.

*****

By having an honest conversation about their financial limits and what they truly need, Sarah and David are able to find a home that works for both of them—without sacrificing their other financial goals.

Saving for Kids, Retirement, and Everything in Between

When you're building a life together, the list of things to save for can feel endless. There's having kids, preparing for retirement, maybe buying a home, and all the other big life events that fall in between. Juggling all of these priorities can feel overwhelming, but with a little planning, it's possible to make steady progress on each one.

The first thing to recognize is that not everything needs to be tackled at once. It's important to prioritize based on where you are in life and what's most pressing. For example, if starting a family is on the horizon, saving for childcare, education, and medical expenses might take priority. On the other hand, if retirement is closer, building up your nest egg could become the main focus. It's about making sure you're addressing both short-term and long-term goals without feeling like you're drowning in financial obligations.

It's also key to remember that life doesn't happen in neat, predictable stages. You might be saving for your future child's education while also thinking about putting money away for your own retirement. That's why it's important to be flexible. Saving for multiple goals at once is tricky, but dividing your income into specific buckets can help. A certain percentage might go toward retirement savings, another portion toward future kids or a house, and some toward everyday expenses and fun.

Retirement might feel far off, especially if you're in the middle of other major life changes, but it's one area where starting early can make a huge difference. By consistently putting aside money in retirement accounts like a 401(k) or IRA, even in small amounts, you're allowing compound interest to work in your favor over time. You don't have to max out these accounts right away, but contributing regularly is a smart way to ensure that future you will be taken care of.

When it comes to saving for kids, the expenses can add up quickly—everything from diapers to daycare to eventually saving for college. Some couples choose to open savings accounts or college funds, like a 529 plan, even before their kids are born. It's never too early to plan for these future costs, but it's also okay to take it one step at a time. You don't have to have it all figured out immediately.

Life throws curveballs, and sometimes you'll have to shift your focus. An unexpected job loss or medical expense might mean hitting pause on one goal to address another more urgent need. The key is to stay adaptable and keep communicating with your partner. As long as you're both on the same page, you can adjust your savings plan without feeling like you've failed.

No couple can save for everything at once, but by being thoughtful and strategic about where your money goes, you can feel confident that you're making progress. Whether it's saving for kids, retirement, or something else entirely, the goal is to build a future that feels secure, without losing sight of the life you're enjoying today.

The Unexpected: Budgeting for Emergencies and Surprises

Life has a way of throwing curveballs when you least expect them, and that's especially true when it comes to money. Whether it's an unexpected medical bill, a car breakdown, or an emergency home repair, these surprises can easily derail your budget if you're not prepared. That's why setting aside money for the unexpected is one of the most important financial habits any couple can develop.

Creating an emergency fund isn't just a "nice-to-have"; it's essential. The goal is to build up enough savings to cover at least three to six months of living expenses. It sounds like a lot, and it can be overwhelming at first, but the idea is to start small and build over time. Setting aside even a little bit each month can make a huge difference when an emergency strikes. Knowing you have a financial cushion helps reduce stress and keeps you from reaching for a credit card when the unexpected happens.

It's also important to remember that emergencies aren't always big disasters. They can be smaller surprises too—like needing to replace your phone after it breaks or covering a sudden vet bill for your pet. These things may not seem like a big deal in the moment, but without a plan, they can start to pile up and strain your finances.

One way to stay prepared is to make budgeting for the unexpected a regular part of your financial routine. Every month, set aside a portion of your income specifically for emergencies. Even if you don't use it right away, it's there when you need it, and you'll thank yourself later. This also keeps you from feeling guilty about dipping into savings for those unplanned expenses.

As a couple, it's key to be on the same page about what counts as an emergency. Is it a car repair, a medical bill, or something else entirely? Having that conversation ahead of time can prevent misunderstandings and make sure you're both comfortable with how the emergency fund is being used.

Budgeting for surprises isn't about living in fear of what could happen. It's about feeling confident and secure, knowing you're ready for whatever life throws your way. When an emergency pops up, it's easier to tackle the issue with a clear head because you've already set money aside. That peace of mind is priceless, and it allows you to focus on solving the problem, rather than worrying about how to pay for it.

Planning for the unexpected gives you a sense of control, even when life feels unpredictable. And as a couple, it strengthens your ability to navigate challenges together, without letting financial stress get in the way.

Chapter 7

Handling Financial Setbacks Together

Coping with Job Loss or Income Reduction

Facing a job loss or a reduction in income can be one of the most challenging experiences for individuals and couples alike. The initial shock can feel overwhelming, and the uncertainty about the future can create a sense of anxiety that permeates everyday life. However, how you cope with this setback can define your resilience and strengthen your relationship during tough times.

The first step is to acknowledge your feelings. It's normal to feel a mix of emotions—fear, anger, and sadness are all part of the process. Allowing yourself to feel these emotions is essential rather than pushing them aside. It's also important to communicate openly with your partner about what you're experiencing. Sharing your feelings can help both of you feel supported and understood. You're in this together, and expressing vulnerabilities can deepen your bond.

Once you've given yourselves some time to process the situation, it's time to focus on practical steps. Start by assessing your financial situation. Take a good look at your savings, monthly expenses, and any outstanding debts. This doesn't mean you have to create a detailed budget right away, but understanding where you stand financially can help ease some of the anxiety. You may need to adjust your spending temporarily, prioritizing essential expenses while cutting back on non-essentials.

Creating a plan together can provide a sense of control. Discuss what adjustments you both need to make in the short term. Maybe it means postponing a vacation or being more mindful about dining out. Having these conversations can help you feel like you're in sync, tackling challenges as a team rather than feeling isolated or unsupported.

While it's easy to focus solely on the immediate financial impacts, try to think long-term as well. Consider what this job loss might mean for your career trajectory. Could it be an opportunity to explore new fields, pursue a passion, or even go back to school? Sometimes, setbacks can lead to unexpected opportunities. Supporting each other in exploring new job prospects or training can help you both stay motivated and positive.

If the job search takes longer than anticipated, don't hesitate to lean on your support network. Friends, family, or even professional networks can be invaluable resources during tough times. They may have leads on job openings or provide moral support, which can help ease the burden you're feeling.

Throughout this process, it's essential to take care of your mental and emotional well-being. Engage in activities that bring you joy and reduce stress, whether that's going for walks, reading, or spending quality time with loved ones. Maintaining a sense of normalcy can help you both cope with the uncertainty.

Coping with job loss or income reduction isn't easy, but facing it together can help you emerge stronger. By openly communicating, adjusting your financial plans, and supporting each other, you can navigate this difficult period and find new opportunities for growth and resilience.

How to Support Each Other Through Financial Stress

Financial stress can feel like a heavy weight on a relationship, making everything from dinner conversations to weekend plans feel strained. When money gets tight or unexpected expenses pop up, it's easy to feel overwhelmed. But the good news is that you can tackle this challenge together and even come out stronger on the other side.

Start by having an open chat about how you're both feeling. It's completely normal to feel anxious or even scared about money, but keeping those feelings to yourself can lead to misunderstandings. So, find a moment when you can sit down and share your worries. Whether it's about job security, debt, or rising costs, talking it out helps both of you understand each other better. You might be surprised at how much lighter it feels to express those concerns out loud.

Next, take a team approach to the situation. Instead of pointing fingers at each other for past spending decisions, focus on the facts. Sit down together and take a good look at your finances. Go through your budget, list your debts, and figure out where you can make adjustments. Working side by side makes it clear that you're both in this together, which can take a lot of the pressure off.

Once you've assessed your situation, come up with a game plan. Brainstorm ways to tackle the financial challenges ahead. This could mean cutting back on dining out or looking for ways to bring in extra income. Maybe it's time to reach out to a financial advisor for some expert insight. Having a clear plan in place can make a huge difference and help both of you feel more in control of the situation.

Emotional support is just as vital during these times. Financial stress can really wear you down, so make sure to lift each other up. Celebrate small victories—like sticking to your budget or knocking out a payment—because every little bit counts. Acknowledging progress, no matter how minor, keeps the motivation alive and reinforces the idea that you're in this together.

It's also worth noting that money discussions can sometimes lead to tension. If you feel tempers flaring, it's totally okay to take a breather and revisit the conversation later. Walking away when emotions are high can be a smart move, allowing you to come back with a clearer mindset and a fresh perspective.

Don't forget to take care of yourselves, too. Financial stress can be draining, so finding time for self-care is essential. Whether it's a relaxing walk, binge-watching your favorite show, or diving into a hobby, make sure to recharge. Those little moments of joy can make a big difference in your outlook.

Supporting each other through financial stress is really about more than just numbers; it's about nurturing your bond. Open communication, teamwork, and emotional encouragement can help you navigate these challenges and come out the other side feeling even more connected.

Revisiting the Budget in Tough Times

When tough times hit—whether it's a job loss, unexpected medical bills, or something else that shakes up your financial stability—it's easy to feel overwhelmed. But these moments are when it's most important to take a step back and revisit your budget together. It's not always easy, but adjusting how you manage money can make things a little less stressful and help you get through it as a team.

The first thing to do is look at where your money is going right now. Pull up your bank statements, look at your spending, and figure out what's absolutely essential. Things like rent or mortgage, groceries, and utilities obviously need to stay on the list, but maybe some of the extras—like streaming services or dining out—can be cut back, at least for a little while. This is where being honest and realistic with each other comes into play. You both need to agree on what's necessary and what can wait.

Then, there's the question of savings. If you have an emergency fund, now might be the time to dip into it. That's what it's there for, after all. If you don't have one, it's a good opportunity to start building one, even if it's just putting a small amount aside whenever possible. Every bit helps.

You'll also want to check if there are any debts you're juggling. It's okay to make adjustments here too. You might look into contacting creditors to see if they offer any temporary relief, like lower payments or deferred interest. It's better to reach out and ask for options than to let things snowball.

And let's not forget to give each other some grace during this process. It's stressful trying to figure out how to make everything work, and tensions can rise quickly when money is tight. But tackling it together, making decisions as a team, can strengthen your bond. Being in it together makes the challenges feel less isolating.

Things may not be easy for a while, and that's okay. Budgets aren't set in stone—they're meant to change and adapt when life throws something unexpected your way. What matters most is that you're flexible, willing to adjust, and committed to working through it as a couple.

Knowing When It's Time to Reward Yourselves

Managing money as a couple can feel like a constant balancing act. You're saving, budgeting, paying off debts, and working toward long-term goals, all while trying to live your everyday life. But somewhere in that mix, it's easy to forget the importance of taking a step back and rewarding yourselves for all the hard work.

It's not just about surviving financially—it's about celebrating the small wins along the way. Maybe you've finally paid off a credit card or hit a big savings milestone. These moments deserve recognition. Treating yourselves to something special, whether it's a nice dinner, a weekend getaway, or even just a new gadget you've been eyeing, can keep you motivated. It's a way of acknowledging that, yes, you've been sticking to your financial plan, and that deserves to be celebrated.

That said, finding the right time to reward yourselves is about balance. You don't want to undo the progress you've made by splurging too much too soon. But waiting forever to enjoy the fruits of your labor can leave you feeling burnt out and deprived. It's okay to indulge a little as long as it fits within your budget and doesn't throw you off track.

For some couples, it's helpful to plan these rewards in advance. Set aside a portion of your income specifically for something fun. That way, when you hit a milestone, you've already built in room to celebrate without guilt or stress.

Rewarding yourselves doesn't have to be extravagant, either. Even small, thoughtful gestures can serve as a reminder that all your effort is paying off. Whether it's dinner at your favorite restaurant, a spontaneous day trip, or simply spending time together doing something you love, these rewards create positive reinforcement.

Taking time to enjoy these moments gives you the energy and motivation to keep moving forward. It's not just about financial progress—it's about enjoying the journey and making sure you feel good about the effort you're putting in.

Conclusion

The Peace of Mind That Comes with Financial Harmony

When you and your partner find a rhythm with your finances, it's more than just having numbers line up—it's about feeling secure, less stressed, and more connected. Financial harmony doesn't mean you'll agree on everything or never have the occasional tough conversation about money, but it does mean you're on the same page, working toward the same goals together.

When you know where your money is going, when you can both trust that you've got each other's backs, it brings a sense of calm to your relationship. There's less worry about the next bill, fewer arguments about spending, and more room for focusing on the things that really matter—whether that's traveling, raising a family, or simply enjoying each other's company.

Financial harmony gives you the freedom to live your lives with less worry and more joy. It allows you to tackle life's challenges together, from saving for big dreams to managing everyday expenses, knowing that you've built a foundation of trust and understanding. And that sense of security, knowing you're both steering in the same direction, makes everything else feel a little bit easier.

Trust, Communication, and the Power of Shared Goals

At the heart of every strong financial partnership are three key ingredients: trust, communication, and shared goals. Trust is what allows both partners to feel confident that decisions are being made in the best interest of the relationship, whether it's a big purchase or small everyday spending. Without trust, even the simplest financial decisions can lead to friction.

Communication is what keeps that trust alive. Open, honest conversations about money—whether it's discussing savings, debt, or future plans—help prevent misunderstandings and ensure both people are on the same page. It's not just about how much money you have, but how you both feel about spending, saving, and what really matters to you as a couple.

And then there's the power of shared goals. When you both have a clear vision of what you want to achieve together, it makes all the budgeting, saving, and planning feel purposeful. Whether you're saving for a house, planning a dream vacation, or preparing for retirement, those shared goals give you something to work toward as a team. They make the tough financial decisions easier because you know you're building something bigger together.

It's that combination—trust, open communication, and a sense of working toward the same goals—that creates a strong, financially healthy relationship. It brings you closer, helps you handle challenges, and makes the good times even sweeter.

www.ingramcontent.com/pod-product-compliance
Lightning Source LLC
Chambersburg PA
CBHW050316230526
45471CB00005B/2211